STEM Today

WAR AND THE MILITARY

JOHN PERRITANO

LIGHTBOX
openlightbox.com

LIGHTBOX

Go to **www.openlightbox.com** and enter this book's unique code.

ACCESS CODE

LBXQ7433

Lightbox is an all-inclusive digital solution for the teaching and learning of curriculum topics in an original, groundbreaking way. Lightbox is based on National Curriculum Standards.

STANDARD FEATURES OF LIGHTBOX

AUDIO High-quality narration using text-to-speech system

ACTIVITIES Printable PDFs that can be emailed and graded

SLIDESHOWS Pictorial overviews of key concepts

VIDEOS Embedded high-definition video clips

WEBLINKS Curated links to external, child-safe resources

TRANSPARENCIES Step-by-step layering of maps, diagrams, charts, and timelines

INTERACTIVE MAPS Interactive maps and aerial satellite imagery

QUIZZES Ten multiple choice questions that are automatically graded and emailed for teacher assessment

KEY WORDS Matching key concepts to their definitions

STEM Today

WAR AND THE MILITARY

CONTENTS

THAT'S WAR AND THE MILITARY

In 2019, the budget for the U.S. military was **$6.8 billion**.

With nearly **1 million** soldiers, China has the world's largest army.

In 2018, **16 percent** of U.S. Army personnel were women.

F-16 Fighting Falcons took part in operations over Yugoslavia. More than 25 countries still use them today.

Nothing can be more alarming to soldiers in battle than an enemy they cannot see. So it was in the skies over war-torn Yugoslavia in the late 1990s when two bat-winged airplanes seemingly appeared out of nowhere. The planes' mission was to drop satellite-guided bombs on Serbian forces waging war against the people of Kosovo. These weren't ordinary warplanes. They were American-made B-2 Stealth bombers.

The B-2s were a marvel of science. Engineers shaped the B-2 body to scatter radar signals. Radar sends out beams of **electromagnetic** waves called microwaves. When those waves hit an aircraft, they bounce back to the radar. A radar operator can then tell where the plane is and how fast it is moving. Without any sharp edges or angles, radar signals skipped off the B-2 like a stone on water. The plane's builders also coated the bomber with a special material to absorb the microwaves. The aircraft worked flawlessly. Since then, B-2s have flown in every major U.S. military campaign, including recent wars in Afghanistan and Iraq.

Wars have served for centuries as a means for technological change and scientific innovation. Bows and arrows replaced spears and rocks. Swords evolved from knives and daggers. Guns morphed from single-shot muskets to rapid-fire automatic weapons. Scientists, inventors, and engineers still use their talents to solve the problems of warfare.

The black holes on either side of a B-2's cockpit are air intakes for its jet engines.

TIMELINE

Human beings have always been at war. Whether it be over territory, religion, or some other disagreement, there are always at least two opposing forces and opposing militaries. The fields of science, technology, engineering, and math, or STEM, have always been a major contributor to military successes.

Gunpowder is invented in China by Tang Dynasty alchemists.

850

1155

In Tortona, Italy, Emperor Frederick I Barbarossa puts human bodies in water wells to poison the water as a form of biological warfare.

1776

The first version of a submarine is used during the American Revolutionary War.

1911

A bomb is dropped from an aircraft for the first time in history. The bomb was dropped by an Italian soldier during the Italo-Turkish War in Libya.

1916

The tank is invented in Great Britain. It is first used by the British during World War I.

1945

The first nuclear bomb is successfully tested in Alamogordo, New Mexico. A version of this bomb would later be dropped on Hiroshima, Japan during World War II.

1997

The Chemical Weapons Convention is signed. This treaty bans the use, creation, or stockpiling of any type of chemical weapons.

2018

Nations spend more than $4.9 billion producing Unmanned Aerial Vehicles (UAVs). This number is expected to double by 2027.

1 Science and War and the Military

Gas Attack

Abd al-Mouin took a deep breath. Soon he gasped in pain. The 22-year-old knew what was happening. The house reeked of bleach, the tell-tale sign of chlorine gas. He corralled his nephews and rushed them outside.

The issue of using poison gas created by scientists in warfare has long been controversial.

Every time Mouin inhaled, it felt like his lungs were on fire. Finally, Mouin passed out, his worst fears realized. Mouin and his neighbors living in the Syrian town of Sarmeen were victims of a chlorine gas attack.

Those in the village that day had seen and heard government helicopters flying overhead moments before the noxious fumes wafted across town. Soon, the unmistakable smell of chlorine tumbled down alleyways and into basements. Victims stumbled into clinics searching for relief.

It wasn't the first time the Syrian government had attacked the town with chemicals. "People are so used to it," a rescue worker told *The New York Times*. "We know the sound of a helicopter that goes to a low height and drops a barrel. Nobody has aircraft except the **regime**."

Chemical and biological weapons are often considered to be weapons of mass destruction. This is why much of the world has now banned them.

The attack was one in a string of atrocities that began with the Syrian civil war in 2011. At the time, the people of Syria protested against the brutal government policies of President Bashar al-Assad. In response, Assad cracked down on the "protesters." Although the use of chlorine gas was banned by international treaty in 1925, it didn't stop Assad from unleashing several chemical attacks against rebel-held towns.

In addition to chlorine, the Syrian army also used sarin gas, one of the most dangerous and toxic chemicals on the planet. Sarin—clear, colorless, and tasteless—is a liquid. When sarin hits the air, it turns into a gas. Its effects are similar to an insecticide. Sarin attacks the nervous system, affecting an **enzyme** that acts as an "off switch" in the body. The sarin-soaked enzyme never turns the body's muscles and glands off and they stay constantly stimulated. The gas chokes people to death as they shake uncontrollably.

As a science, chemistry has the power to save lives and make modern living safer and easier. However, it can also be employed by military powers to create weapons for attacking their enemies.

Father of the Gas Attack

The use of chlorine gas was the brainchild of Fritz Haber, a bald and bespectacled German chemist, who took chemistry out of the laboratory and successfully used it on the front lines. In fact, Haber's development of chemical weapons during World War I (1914–18) forever wedded modern science to warfare.

It was April 1915, just outside the Belgian town of Ypres. Haber had traveled to the front lines to supervise the placement of 5,730 chlorine gas cylinders along a stretch of road. At the time, most German generals weren't convinced that poison gas could be an effective weapon. Haber wanted to prove them wrong. At 5:30 p.m. on April 22, with the wind blowing just right, German soldiers wearing gas masks opened the valves on the chlorine tanks. The gas hit the air and, according to a Canadian soldier, a "greenish-yellow fog that seemed strangely out of

Some gases used by German forces during World War I had a blinding effect.

place in the bright atmosphere of that clear April day" crawled over the battlefield.

At first, French troops watched as the green mist wound its way across the trenches. They then looked on in horror as their comrades grabbed their throats in agony. The gas felt like "red-hot needles in the lungs," said one soldier. The gas attacked the respiratory system, obstructing airways. Soldiers wheezed and coughed. Many fell dead.

In regions where a chemical attack is possible, soldiers carry the gear necessary to survive an attack.

Others stumbled out of the trenches seeking escape. Haber couldn't have been more pleased. The gas attack ravaged two French divisions, creating a huge gap in the front lines. "What we saw was total death," one German soldier said. "Nothing was alive. You could see where men had clawed at their faces and throats, trying to get breath. Some had shot themselves."

A similar scene was played out a century later in Syria. After several deadly gas attacks in 2013—including one that killed more than 1,000 people in rebel-held areas near Damascus—international pressure forced Assad to stop using chemical weapons. However, as *The New York Times* reported in 2015, the attacks continued. On March 16, 2015, a bomb shelter in Sarmeen filled with gas, killing a family of six, including three children.

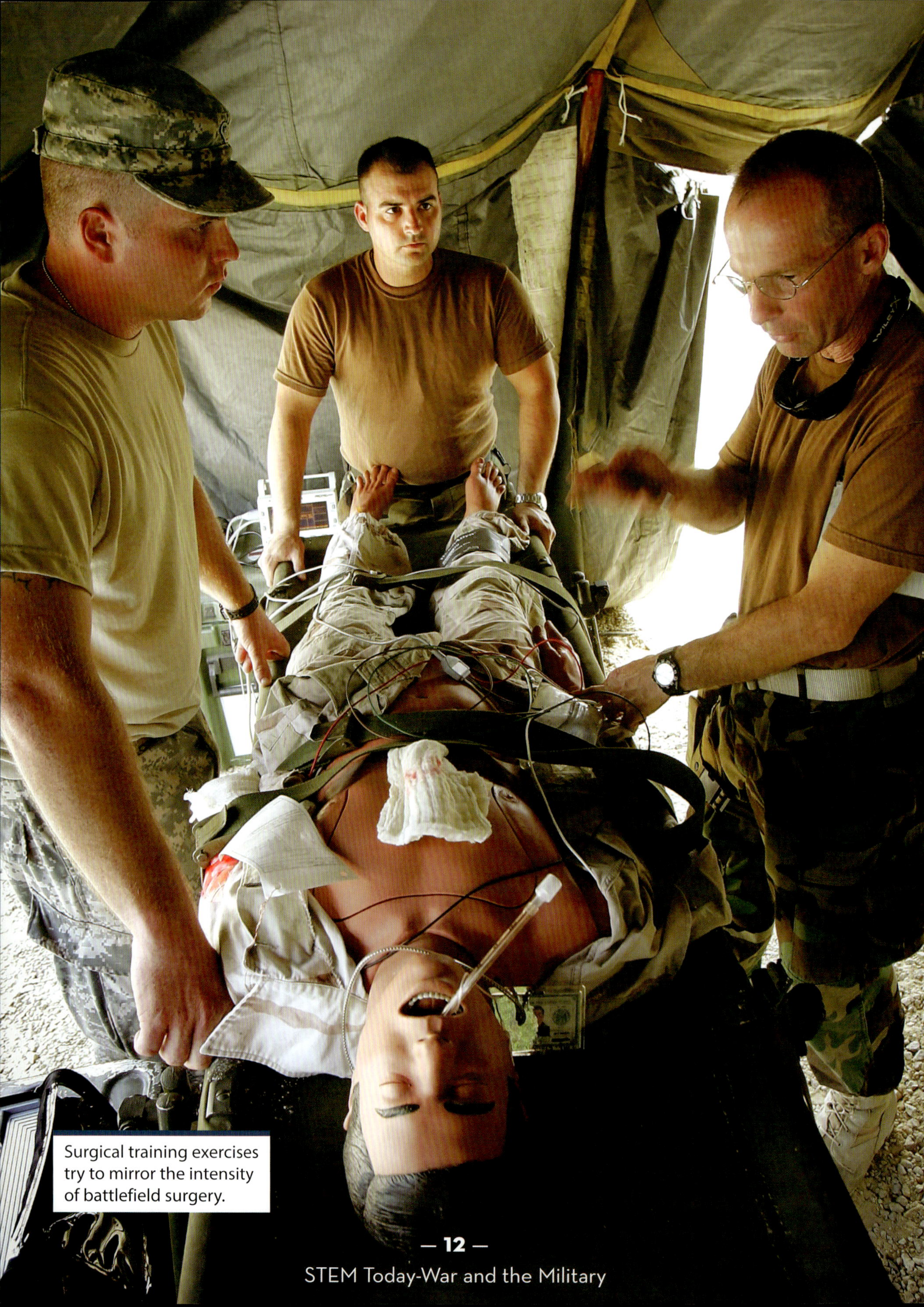
Surgical training exercises try to mirror the intensity of battlefield surgery.

Saving Lives

While science can be used to deadly effect in war, it can also be life saving, especially for soldiers. Being wounded, often seriously, is one of the many horrors of war. Scientists and doctors have worked to find new ways to help injured soldiers survive their wounds. In fact, as wars have evolved, new life-saving discoveries have been made that have proved beneficial to all.

For example, military scientists have found a way to stop the bleeding of abdominal wounds, the gravest injuries a soldier can experience. Doctors can now inject a foam that surrounds the injured organ and slows the internal bleeding. The foam is a type of polyurethane, a human-made plastic. It starts as two liquids that medics inject into the wound. The liquids combine to create a strong and flexible barrier.

The foam expands to nearly 30 times its original volume before solidifying. It seals the wounded tissue, plugging the flow of blood. Doctors can later remove the foam and repair the injury.

Portable Scanners

Scientists have brought the latest medical devices, including CT scanners and ultrasound machines, to the front lines. CT scans, also known as computerized tomography, use digital technology to create a three-dimensional X-ray inside a person's body. Ultrasound machines, also known as diagnostic sonography, use high-frequency sound waves to create images of a patient's organs.

CT and sonogram images from portable machines on the battlefield or at a forward aid station can be sent over the internet to specialists thousands of miles away. Within moments, doctors can make recommendations about treating a patient's wounds. Moreover, front line doctors can send the patient's electronic medical records to the hospital where the soldier will end up.

Anesthetic

Anesthetics were not used on the battlefield until the U.S. Civil War (1861–65). Before that, injured soldiers were told to bite down on a leather strap or a cloth and deal with the pain as best they could. Most passed out when the doctor sawed through skin, muscle, and bone to amputate, or cut off, a limb.

However, in 1847, Scottish physician Sir James Young Simpson found he could use chloroform to render people unconscious. The liquid, slowly dripped into a cloth placed over the patient's nose, affected the nervous system.

Chloroform, however, was dangerous to use. As years passed, scientists developed better drugs. Today, soldiers are given anesthetics **intravenously**. Some are "local" anesthetics that block the central nervous system. The drugs seep into the center chamber of nerve cells

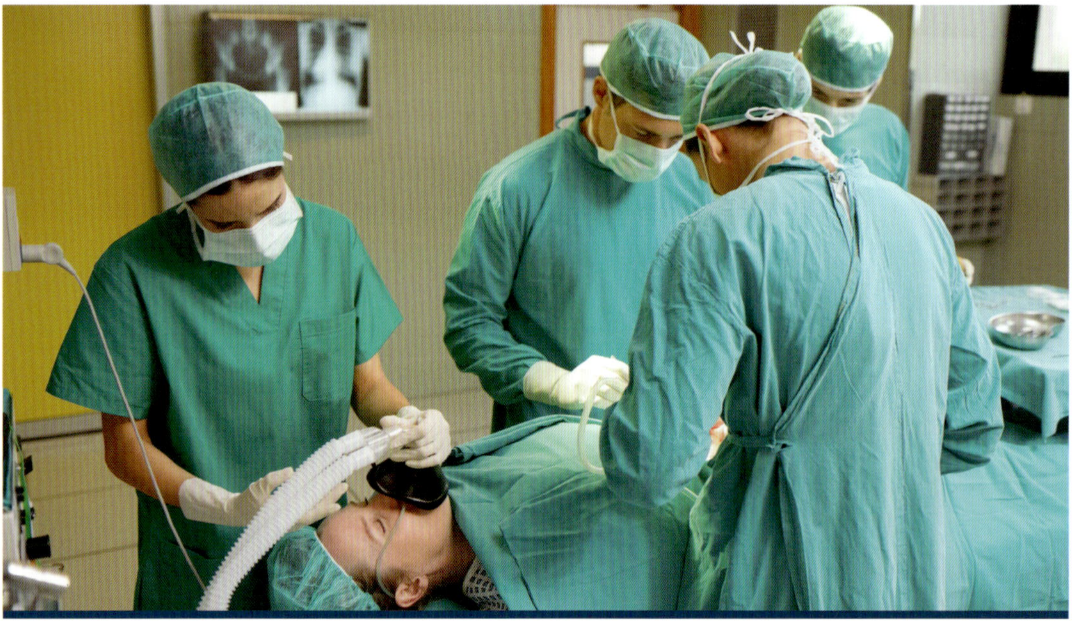

The anesthetics that we now use for even routine medical procedures are a fairly recent invention in the overall history of medicine.

forcing the nerves to stop transmitting pain signals to the brain.

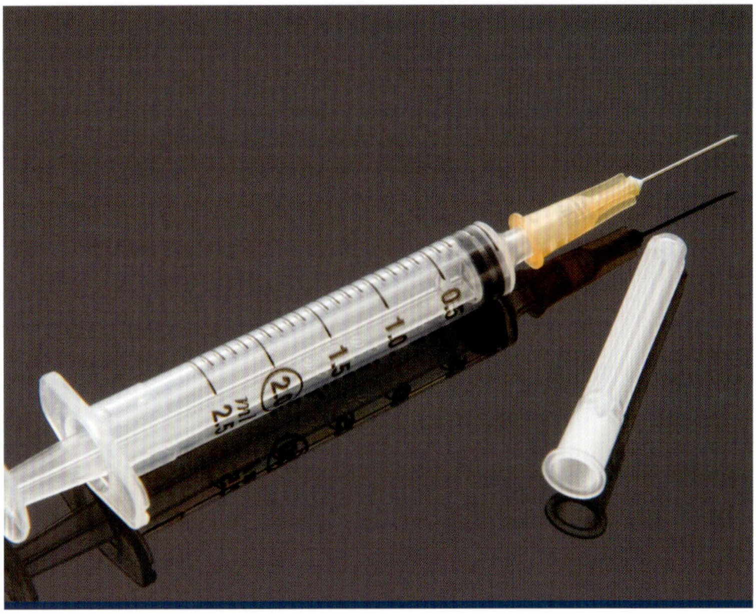
Anesthetics can be injected as well as inhaled.

General anesthetics are another painkiller widely used in battle. The drugs stop the transmission of electrical signals from one neuron to another through tiny intersections known as synapses.

"Regional" anesthetics are the newest development. Doctors used them with great success during the U.S. war with Iraq, which began in 2003. In 2004, Brian Wilhelm was the first wounded soldier to be given a "regional" anesthetic in battle.

A rocket-propelled grenade had ripped the back of his leg. Doctors injected the anesthetic directly into Wilhelm's leg. The drug acted as "nerve blocker." It deadened groups of nerves in the leg called ganglion.

Wilhelm was awake while doctors treated his injury. "He was interacting with his buddies," recalled Army Lt. Col. Chester C. Buckenmaier, who administered the groundbreaking anesthetic. "It was a happy time, rather than a sorrowful time like it usually is after a general anesthetic, where patients are groggy and feel so bad about what's happened to them, and you can't really talk to them. The first time we used regional anesthesia on the battlefield was a very powerful moment."

2 Technology and War and the Military

Defense Advanced Research Projects Agency (DARPA)

When U.S. troops invaded Iraq in 2003, they were thrown into a noisy, chaotic, and dangerous situation. The enemy retreated into the cities and took up positions in buildings and on rooftops. There, they waited for the Americans to appear. As soon as U.S. troops walked into view, the snipers pulled the trigger, killing and wounding many.

The 2003 conflict in Iraq led to several advances in military gear.

Snipers also took aim as armor-plated Humvees rolled down the street. It was so loud inside the boxlike armored vehicles that those inside could not hear the gunshots. Even when soldiers knew they were under fire, they had no idea where the bullets came from.

Something had to be done—and fast. Military planners rushed to develop a sniper-protection system. They enlisted the help of researchers at the Defense Advanced Research Projects Agency (DARPA).

DARPA has been providing the U.S. military with cutting-edge technology since the 1950s.

The High Mobility Multipurpose Wheeled Vehicle (Humvee) is a key part of the U.S. military.

In 66 days, DARPA scientists and other researchers invented Boomerang, an electronic sniper-detection device. At the heart of Boomerang was a cluster of microphones mounted on a 9-foot (2.75-meter) aluminum pole. Soldiers attached the pole to the top of their armored vehicles.

The microphones listened for the sound made by a sniper's rifle and the shockwaves created by a speeding bullet hurtling through the air. A computer then analyzed the data in less than a second. It correctly pinpointed where the shot came from. It also zeroed in on how high up the shooter was.

The device displayed the information on a screen inside the vehicle. A computerized voice also alerted soldiers and told them where to look. "This is what I would want on every Humvee if my child was out there," said one DARPA official.

The average speed of a sound wave in air is **767 miles** (1,234 kilometers) **per hour**.

Emile Berliner invented the world's first microphone in **1876.**

As of 2019, the world record for a successful sniper shot was **11, 614 feet** (3,540 m).

Changing Technology

When armies march into battle, the side that has a technological edge often has the advantage. The ancient Egyptians, for example, built the horse-drawn chariot so they could move quickly across the battlefield. When medieval armies sought sanctuary inside the walls of castles, weapon-makers invented the catapult to knock down the walls.

In the 20th century, fighter planes, artillery, and mechanized tanks were technological marvels that changed the course of modern war. These days, soldiers use a variety of sophisticated weapons and devices. Some are straight out of science fiction.

In the old days of combat, calling in an air strike to destroy an enemy's position took time. A soldier had to look at a map, write down the enemy's position, and phone in the strike.

In June 2013, soldiers started using a device called the Advanced Warfighter Awareness for Real-time Engagement system. Known as AWARE, the system allowed a soldier to target the enemy by simply looking through a high-tech **monocle** mounted on his or her helmet. The device automatically sent the target's coordinates to

From the earliest days of human conflict, technology has played a vital role. A catapult was "state of the art" in ancient times.

Soldiers use battle-ready smartphones and other communications tools to link up with a wide variety of information.

a fighter jet or an armored vehicle, which then carried out the strike.

Helmets have also gone high-tech. British researchers invented a new bulletproof helmet with night-vision goggles and a camera. The camera can send real-time battlefield images to commanders far away. Officers can then see what is happening in the thick of the fight.

Finding an electrical outlet on the battlefield to charge smartphones, Global Positioning Systems (GPS), and other gadgets is difficult. Scientists solved the problem by stitching together a solar-powered uniform. The uniform absorbs power from the Sun during the day. At night, it uses the heat of a soldier's body to generate electricity. The uniform provides troops with a continuous supply of electricity to power devices, including weapon systems.

Scientists at the Engineering and Physical Research Sciences Center in Great Britain came up with the idea. They put **photovoltaic** cells into the uniform. The electricity produced by the cells could then be stored in lightweight batteries. As an added benefit, solar uniforms made a soldier safer. Since the fabric absorbs body heat, a soldier is less likely to be detected by an enemy's **infrared** camera.

Heavy Lifting

Carrying heavy loads across a battlefield can be grueling and tiresome. In 2010, engineers at Lockheed Martin took a page from the world of army ants to create the Human Universal Load Carrier (HULC). The HULC works like an ant's **exoskeleton**, helping soldiers carry up to 200 pounds (90 kilograms) by transferring the stress of the weight to the ground.

The device attaches to a soldier's hips and boots. It acts as a mechanical, battery-operated spine. HULC's computer tells the device to match the movement and direction of its user.

HULC can crawl, climb, and jog. It also helps soldiers to march up to eight hours without losing a charge. This technology is relatively new, but smart technology has been improving defense strategies for hundreds of years.

An ant can carry 5,000 times its body weight.

Weapons Upgrade

On January 17, 1991, the United States and its allies attacked Iraq, weeks after the Iraqi army had invaded Kuwait. The first weapons fired were super-smart missiles launched from warships hundreds of miles away. The computer-guided weapons hit their targets with pinpoint accuracy. The most important was the Tomahawk cruise missile. The missile flew 550 miles (885 km) per hour 100 feet (30 m) above the ground, making it invisible to enemy radar. Also in the air that day were F-117 stealth fighters. The sleek aircraft, also invisible to radar, dropped smart bombs guided by computer brains on hundreds of military targets.

It could be said that the Gulf War, also known as Operation Desert Storm, was the world's first high-tech war. Laser-guided weapons, computerized missile defense systems, tanks that used **depleted uranium** armor for protection, and airborne robots ruled the day. The results were stunning. The Iraqi army crumbled in just over 30 days. Allied forces freed Kuwait. The success of the war ushered in a new era of high-tech warfare and research.

Smart Bullet

In 2012, researchers at the Sandia National Laboratories unveiled the world's first "smart bullet," a self-guided projectile that can hit a target more than a mile away. The bullet's brain has an optical sensor that can see the red dot of a laser beam pointed at a target. Electromagnetic fins steer the bullet as it zips through the air. Like a guided missile, the bullet moves left, right, up, and down as it hones in on its target. The bullet is so smart that it can change direction in mid-flight. However, scientists still have to tweak the smart bullet. It moves 600 feet (200 m) per second slower than a regular rifle bullet.

A laser cannon aboard a U.S. Navy warship can be used for defense by firing at targets such as enemy missiles or oncoming airplanes.

Laser Fighters

In a scene straight out of a science fiction movie, the U.S. Air Force is planning to put laser cannons on fighter planes. It's hard to do. The system has to be small enough to be mounted on the outside of the airplanes.

It's not the first time the Air Force has experimented with high-flying ray guns. In the mid-1990s and early 2000s, scientists experimented with a laser generated by a chemical reaction between chlorine, hydrogen peroxide, and potassium hydroxide. The device was too big, however, and was not useful.

The U.S. Navy is also testing a laser cannon aboard some of its ships. The first tests didn't go well. But scientists say such "directed energy" weapons can be put on tanks and even unmanned balloons. The laser cannons would fire a high-energy light beam that can destroy an enemy ship, truck, or tank.

Other weapons have some interesting effects. In fact, one futuristic weapon might make you sick to your stomach. A U.S. company has developed a weapon called the Dazer Laser. The device is as big as a flashlight and uses a green laser beam that makes people sick to their stomachs.

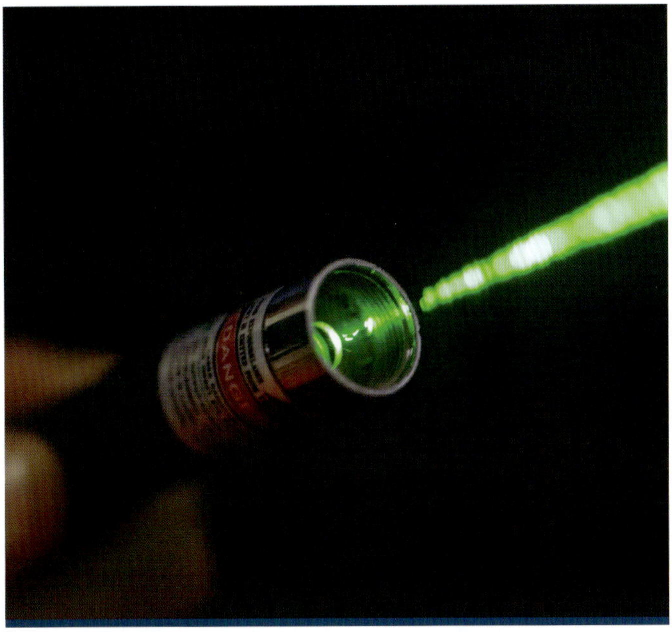

Laser stands for Light Amplification by Stimulated Emission of Radiation.

Online Mayhem

While scientists work feverishly to build new weapons, they are also trying to defend against cyber attacks. In recent years, the governments of countries such as China, Russia, and North Korea have used the internet to break into a number of computer systems.

In 2014, the U.S. government implicated North Korea in a devastating cyber attack on Sony Pictures. Many believe the North Koreans were also behind a crippling attack on South Korean computer systems.

Infrastructures and physical systems linked to the internet are targets of cyber warfare. To combat this, the U.S. military has developed significant cyber capabilities.

Since computers are an important part of a nation's transportation, economic, and banking systems, a hacker can infect computer systems and networks with viruses. Harming these systems could wreak social and economic havoc. In response, many nations are working to build sophisticated computer defenses to stop the attacks.

Moreover, some nations, including the United States, are taking cyber warfare to the next level. Scientists have developed e-bombs, or electronic bombs, that can blast an enemy's computer system with high-energy bursts of microwaves—the same invisible energy found in microwave ovens. The bombs can fry the computer system and other electronic devices.

LIMITS OF TECHNOLOGY IN WARFARE

Technology has its limits in warfare, especially when the enemy can find ways around it or the terrain makes it fail. There have been many examples of these limits as war and weapons have evolved.

World War I: German soldiers dug trenches as a way to move forward in battle. The British then used tanks to overcome the barriers. The success of the tanks gave rise to anti-tank artillery and missiles.

1

World War II: From World War II on, the tactical advantage of air power was minimized by radar, anti-aircraft defense systems, and surface-to-air missiles. To overcome those defenses, researchers built aircraft and weapons that were more sophisticated, including smart bombs, and satellite-guided missiles.

2

3

Vietnam War: The jungle warfare required in the Vietnam War was a new, technological challenge for the U.S. military. Hit-and-run attacks by the Viet Cong reduced the effectiveness of conventional U.S. weaponry and tactics.

Iraq War: The United States deployed many high-tech weapons and devices, including robotic drones and satellite vehicle-tracking systems that marked the location of U.S. fighting units. However, some computers broke down. In Iraq, downloads took hours. Software locked. The breakdowns disrupted digital communication.

4

3 Engineering and War and the Military

Bulletproof Buildings

Nick Boone and his colleagues at the U.S. Army Corps of Engineers had an idea. They knew soldiers in battle adapted to their conditions as best they could. Instead of digging foxholes for protection, for example, troops built makeshift shelters out of pieces of brick, cinder block, and wood. While these buildings offered some measure of protection, a well-placed mortar shell or missile could turn the dwellings into rubble.

Boone, a research engineer at the U.S. Army Engineer Research and Development Center (ERDC) in Vicksburg, Mississippi, thought he could help. In 2015, Boone and other ERDC engineers unveiled a new type of wallpaper they hope will protect soldiers inside their crude shelters. Engineers designed the so-called ballistic wallpaper to catch bits of high-flying rubble and shrapnel.

Creating a defensible space is often the work of combat engineers. They use everything from hand tools to heavy equipment to build whatever their forces need to live and survive.

Made from Kevlar threads attached to a bendable polymer film, ballistic wallpaper is super-strong. ERDC researchers want soldiers to stick the wallpaper on the inside of their shelters. When a mortar shell, grenade, or missile strikes the outside wall, the wallpaper will catch shards of flying debris like a baseball mitt.

Kevlar-laced wallpaper is designed to stop walls from "rubblizing." It was tested by building and then bombing small buildings.

“The idea of coating the inside of structures to reduce the danger of [debris] to occupants is not new,” Justin Bronk, research analyst at the Royal United Services Institute, told the *BBC*. “What appears relatively new about this ballistic wallpaper is that it can be quickly and easily applied by non-specialized units at short notice. This provides significant potential tactical advantages.”

But that’s not all the ERDC has been working on. ERDC engineers also developed a Modular Protective System (MPS). The MPS is made of lightweight super-strong panels that can shield guard towers and mortar pits from enemy fire. Each protective panel is made of multiple layers of fiberglass and steel tubing. Fiberglass is heat- and fire-resistant. Its fibers are woven tightly together like a spider’s web. The MPS is easy to assemble and take apart. It can be stored in a shipping container and moved to different locations.

A series of test explosions proved that the MPS works as built. Engineers detonated charges around the protective wall system. “Other than the damaged zone on the upper roof, the structure is completely reusable, and the covered area is completely protected,” said engineer Omar Flores.

Engineering to Victory

Engineers can turn the tide of a battle. When the Persian Empire, commanded by King Xerxes, went to war with Greece in 480 BC, engineers helped move Xerxes' massive army of 150,000 men, wagons, and horses from Asia Minor to Greece over a tiny ribbon of water called the Dardanelles. The Dardanelles separates Asia Minor from Europe. Engineers built two bridges of boats and linked them together in a 1-mile (1.6-km) chain. It took seven days and seven nights to move Xerxes' army across the bridge.

Today's military engineers use techniques that are more sophisticated. They design and build military bases, harbors, and roads, and also make sure that communication lines remain open.

Combat engineers also help in peacetime. They can help build shelter and provide other services to people in need.

Combat engineers, also called field engineers, work under battle conditions. They clear obstacles from roadways and rivers. They detonate explosives, look for mines, and build floating bridges and defensive positions. Strategic engineers have many jobs, including building airfields and roads, and improving ports.

They also build military barracks that can withstand a direct missile or mortar attack. Most military bases are temporary and are constructed of wooden, brick, and metal structures. When a base becomes a permanent facility, however, engineers create blast-proof buildings that can withstand the punishment of enemy fire.

Most blast-resistant buildings are made of composite metals and columns that can shoulder the impact of a blast. The walls are made with flexible sheeting that bend and deflect debris away from the supporting steel structure. The walls will not crack or fall when hit by a missile or other explosives.

Moreover, engineers design blast-resistant roofs. Some roofs are simple steel grids mounted on poles that will catch the mortar as it falls. The idea is to minimize the energy created by the blast so walls and ceilings do not shatter.

No ancient civilization could match Rome for its engineering know-how. Much of what the Romans built can still be seen today, including *castra*, or garrison towns, protected by large walls and ditches.

Protecting Against IEDs

One of the main jobs of the military engineer is to keep soldiers safe. That was the assignment of one Arizona National Guard unit when it went overseas to Afghanistan. The engineers' job was to look for signs of digging along roadways. They scanned for garbage and other debris that had no place being there. What they were really looking for was evidence of hidden improvised explosive devices (IEDs).

Despite the massive firepower brought to Iraq and Afghanistan by the United States and its allies, IEDs tormented troops, since insurgents could build a

After locating an IED and clearing the area, army engineers may detonate the device rather than try to remove it.

simply constructed device for less than $100. They would hide the bombs anywhere they could, including behind buildings, under roadways, and in trucks. Some IEDs were strapped to suicide bombers.

According to one estimate, nearly half of Americans killed or wounded in combat in Iraq and Afghanistan fell victim to IEDs. The IED's impact changed the way engineers and soldiers did their jobs. "They've caused us a lot of pain... a lot of effort and a lot of treasure," one general told *USA Today*.

Engineers were forced to rethink how to equip and protect soldiers. They installed more armor on vehicles and designed new body-armored suits. As lower legs and feet were most likely to be injured by an exploding IED, they invented armored floor mats and placed them in military vehicles.

Medical engineers designed new computerized prostheses to replace limbs torn off by the blasts. The IED also spurred researchers at a company called Boeing to invent a "force field" to protect vehicles. Engineers studied the explosions caused by IEDs. When an IED explodes, it sends out shards of shrapnel that can injure or kill an unsuspecting soldier. However, the blast also produces deadly shockwaves.

Shockwave Attenuation System

IED shockwaves change the temperature, pressure, and density of the atmosphere. Like a stone thrown into a pond, the massive energy of the shockwave ripples out in circles. The force is so powerful it can kill someone more easily than the fire of a blast. Boeing's force field, or "shockwave attenuation system," uses lasers to zap the air to create an electromagnetic shockwave of its own, shrouding a military vehicle in a protective cocoon. The force field absorbs the energy of the incoming shockwave, minimizing the impact of the IED. The device can also be used on submarines and navy ships.

Engineering on the High Seas

Military engineers also work building, running, and maintaining some of the most sophisticated ships ever built, including nuclear-powered aircraft carriers and submarines. Perhaps one of the greatest engineering marvels on the high seas is the U.S.S. *Nimitz*, a nuclear-powered aircraft carrier that has a flight deck more than four acres—or nearly four football fields long. Nearly 6,000 sailors live aboard the *Nimitz*, which stands about

23 stories high. First commissioned in 1975, the *Nimitz* is named after Admiral Chester W. Nimitz. It is a floating fortress that carries more than 90 aircraft. Powered by two nuclear reactors, the *Nimitz*, and the other carriers in its class, is a "supercarrier." With about one billion individual parts, Nimitz-class carriers are among the most complicated machines on the planet.

It's tough to sink a Nimitz-class carrier. The hull of each ship is engineered with strong steel plates several inches thick. The steel protects the carriers against fire and battle damage.

Each Nimitz-class aircraft carrier cost about $4.5 billion to build.

The lower section of the ship has a double bottom—two layers of steel plating—one right above the other. It protects the carrier from torpedo attacks. Even if one of the explosives penetrates the outside layer, engineers designed the second layer to prevent a leak.

Perhaps one of the unique functions of the Nimitz-class supercarrier is the ability to turn seawater into drinkable water. Engineers can turn seawater into 400,000 gallons (1.6 million liters) of fresh water a day, in a process called desalination. It is essential for nuclear-powered carriers.

Nuclear reactors are always thirsty. That's because the reactors heat water, creating the steam that powers the ship. The reactors cannot use saltwater, only pure water. That's where desalination comes in. Some ships use reverse osmosis to purify salt water. The ships pump the saltwater under tremendous pressure through special cleansing membranes. These filters remove any sediment, bacteria, and viruses from the water. The seawater is then pumped through a series of filters that remove the salt. Once the fresh water is purified, it can be stored and used.

After their ship turns seawater into fresh water, the crew on the U.S.S. *Nimitz* can give the ship's superstructure and deck a cleansing bath with high-pressure hoses.

Living Conditions

Nuclear submarines are super-sophisticated, yet engineers had to design the subs with limited space. The toilets are made from cold stainless steel, food is stacked in every available compartment, and garbage piles up everywhere.

Nearly 150 or so people live and work on the vessels. Submariners don't have their own bedrooms. Instead, they sleep in stacked bunk beds. They do not have dressers or closets. Sailors have to stow their gear in small bins under the bunk.

Although a cramped life can be tough, it's not even close to living in a war torn area. Afghanistan is a war-weary country. Prior to the American-led invasion after the terrorist attacks on September 11, 2001, Afghanistan was a hotbed of tribal warfare. Beginning in 1976, the Soviet Union had spent 12 years fighting the Mujahideen, the guerrilla soldiers led by Muslim Afghan warriors.

All that fighting left the nation in ruins. During the past few years, however, military engineers began piecing the country back together. They have built schools, hospitals, and other buildings damaged by bombing.

They have brought electricity to areas that had none. They have sunk wells for clean water. "I think rebuilding...will have a lot longer impact and a lot more impact than the bombs did," one U.S. soldier told *ABC News*.

Although a war can be officially ended with a peace treaty, the effects on a country and its population can last for decades.

4 Math and War and the Military

Saving a Life

Timothy Gilboe stood before the crowd at the Veterans for Foreign Wars Post in Portland, Maine, and held up the piece of body armor that saved his life in Afghanistan. Gilboe, a sergeant with the 2nd Battalion, 4th Infantry Regiment, 10th Mountain Division, was on patrol with his platoon near the village of Awalata when insurgents attacked.

A firefight took place as Gilboe and his squad moved through the village. One of the bullets killed the squad's leader, Matthew Hermanson. One enemy round struck the rucksack of an assistant machine gunner, setting the bag on fire. Gilboe dropped his gun and put the flames out. But the enemy fighters kept coming. They charged Gilboe's position. With no time to retrieve his gun, Gilboe ran towards one of the insurgents. He grabbed the man's rifle.

Sgt. Timothy Gilboe was saved by a single protective plate. It stopped a bullet that might have killed him during a firefight in Afghanistan.

At one point, the rifle's muzzle was pointed directly into Gilboe's chest. The insurgent pulled the trigger. A bullet ripped into the vest, sending Gilboe backwards.

Yet the bullet did not penetrate the protective layers of the vest. Dazed, but otherwise alright, Gilboe caught his breath and grabbed the enemy fighter, taking his weapon away and punching him in the face.

That gave one of Gilboe's squad members the time to take aim and gun down the enemy combatant. With the attack over, Gilboe tended to several of his injured friends. Several years later, Gilboe stood before Portland's veterans and paid homage to his fallen friend.

The protective plate, covered in bulletproof fabric, was large. Had the vest been smaller, Gilboe might have been killed. "I'm glad they didn't give me a medium," Gilboe said.

Body armor goes by many names, including flak jackets, personal armor, and bulletproof vests. Whatever the soldiers call it, body armor has saved many lives in combat. Although the idea of protective armor goes back centuries, the body armor of today can stop a speeding bullet or projectile dead in its tracks. And the path to creating body armor starts with math.

Catch a Speeding Bullet

To measure the ballistic performance of body armor, scientists have to calculate the kinetic energy of a bullet. Kinetic energy, the energy in motion, depends on not only the bullet's velocity, but also its mass. The mathematical relationship between each is written as follows:

$$\textbf{Kinetic Energy} = \frac{\textbf{Mass} \times \textbf{Velocity}^2}{2}$$

Kinetic energy increases as velocity increases. According to this equation, the kinetic energy of an object is proportional, or relative, to its speed. That means for every twofold increase in the speed of a bullet, the bullet's kinetic energy increases by a factor of four. In other words, the faster a bullet travels, the more kinetic energy it has. The more energy the bullet has, the more damage it can do when it strikes the vest.

Scientists test body armor by shooting it with different types of bullets from various angles. For the armor to be effective, it has to stop a bullet without causing serious injury.

Testing the Math

Once the kinetic energy of a bullet has been determined, scientists use a measurement to determine the velocity in which no bullet can penetrate the armor. Scientists call this "zero penetration velocity," or V0 for short. Many variables affect V0. Those variables include the type of bullet, the type of gunpowder used, the bullet casing, the gun, and the armor itself.

The measurement, however, is an estimate, and difficult to figure out. Scientists have developed a second ballistic measurement called V50. This measures the velocity in which 50 percent of the shots penetrate the target and the other 50 percent do not.

Stopping bullets is just one job of body armor.

The other is to protect against shrapnel. Depending on the explosives, shrapnel can travel up to 30,000 feet (9,144 m) per second. In determining how well an armored vest can stand up to shrapnel, scientists use the 2-4-16-64 test. It is based on the mass of the shrapnel. Most shrapnel fragments are less than 4 grains. Each fragment travels at a velocity of 3,000 feet (914 m) per second.

The average bullet travels at **1,700 miles** (2,736 km) **per hour**.

The first bulletproof vest was invented in **1893** by Casimir Zeglen.

Modern rifles have a muzzle velocity of nearly **4,000 feet** (1,219 m) **per second**.

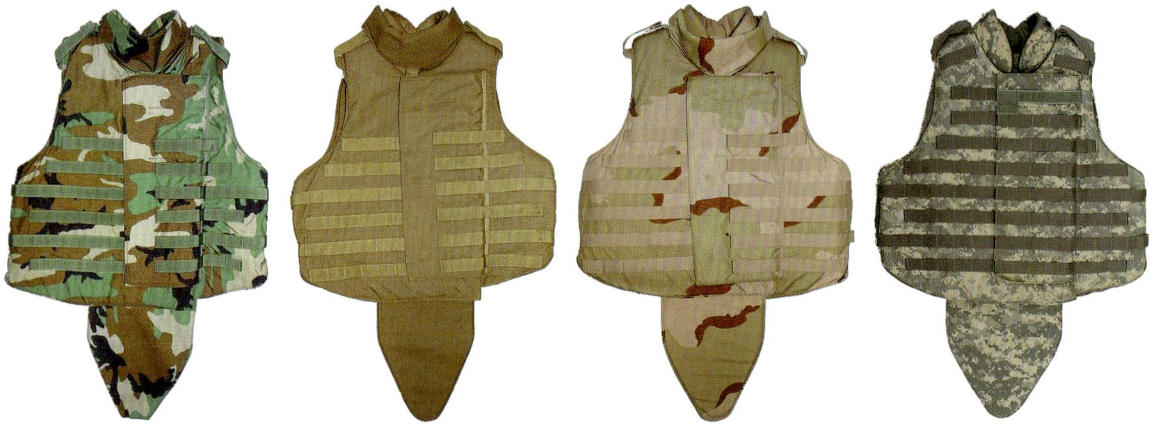

Because soldiers work in different physical environments, the gear that holds their body armor comes in a variety of camouflage styles

The U.S. military certifies all body armor tests into several categories. Category I offers the lowest level of protection, while category IV offers the highest. The lowest level protects against small-caliber bullets, which generate less energy on impact. The highest-level body armor can protect against larger caliber weapons.

Body armor comes in two types, hard and soft. Hard body armor is made out of thick ceramic or metal plates. These plates work the same way as suits of armor worked during medieval times. They deflect an oncoming bullet by pushing out with the same force with which the bullet pushes in.

Soldiers often wear soft body armor. Soft body armor, made from layers of bulletproof fibers, stops a bullet or shell fragment like a hockey net trapping a puck. Like a hockey puck, the incoming bullet has a high amount of energy. When the bullet hits the bulletproof material of an armored vest, the material disperses the bullet's energy over a wide area.

Energy is further dispersed because of the interlocking design of the bulletproof fabric. When the bullet strikes the horizontal fabric, it pulls on the interlaced vertical fabric, scattering the energy over a wider area.

Many types of body armor are made out of Kevlar, which was invented in 1965 by Stephanie Kwolek, a chemist at DuPont. She developed the miracle fabric for use in tires. It was flameproof and light. Kevlar was the perfect fabric to reinforce the thread of radial tires.

Scientists soon discovered that Kevlar could be woven into suits of armor. Its fibers were strong enough to stop most bullets and shrapnel. Many types of body armor are also stuffed with ceramic "trauma plates." The plates protect the area just below the waist. A second plate covers the chest. Kevlar is five times stronger than steel and less dense than fiberglass.

During the Iraq and Afghanistan wars, American and British ground troops—not to mention journalists—first started wearing Kevlar helmets and a 16-pound (7-kg) Kevlar vest with ceramic plates. The vests were designed to stop a number of projectiles, including armor-piercing bullets fired from high-powered rifles. The ceramic plates of these Kevlar vests, known as Interceptor Body Armor, can shatter a bullet.

"Not in a thousand years did I think [the] discovery of [Kevlar] would save thousands of lives," Kwolek once told *USA Today*. "When I watch the war on TV, I take great pride in saying, 'We at DuPont invented that.'"

STEM Saves Lives

Jason Ashline was glad he was wearing a Kevlar vest when he was struck by two bullets from an AK-47 assault rifle. The bullets harmlessly lodged in the vest. "The bullets knocked me over and took the wind out of me, but I didn't feel any pain." Without science, injured soldiers might not have come home. Without technology, snipers might have killed more troops. Without engineering, service personnel might not survive bomb blasts of their buildings. Without math, many soldiers might not be with their loved ones today. STEM, and the products created with that knowledge, saves lives.

STEM AND WAR AND THE MILITARY AROUND THE WORLD

Unfortunately, war and human conflict have been around as long as there have been people. As science evolves, so too do our skills at making more efficient and effective ways to wage war.

1 United States

The U.S. Army training school for chemical, biological, radiological, and nuclear (CBRN) defense is located in Fort Leonard Wood, Missouri. The CBRN school is tasked to both handle and prevent any attacks that all under these categories.

2 Bosnia

On June 28, 1914, Archduke Ferdinand was assassinated in Sarajevo, Bosnia. This assassination started a series of events that would lead to the start of World War I. During this war, Germany became the first country to use chemical weapons in the 20th century.

3 China

Gunpowder was invented in China in the 9th century. This invention would revolutionize warfare. The creation of guns, bombs, and other explosive devices can all be traced back to this important moment in history.

4 Japan

Following the bombing of Hiroshima, the second nuclear bomb of World War II was dropped on Nagasaki, Japan on August 9, 1945. This final attack by the United States forced the Japanese to surrender, ending World War II.

RESEARCH PROJECTS

Science

1. Form two groups. One group should research and argue the merits of military science. The other group should research the negative effects of military research.
1. Hold a debate with your classmates discussing whether or not military research is positive. Be sure to use information from your research to support your arguments.

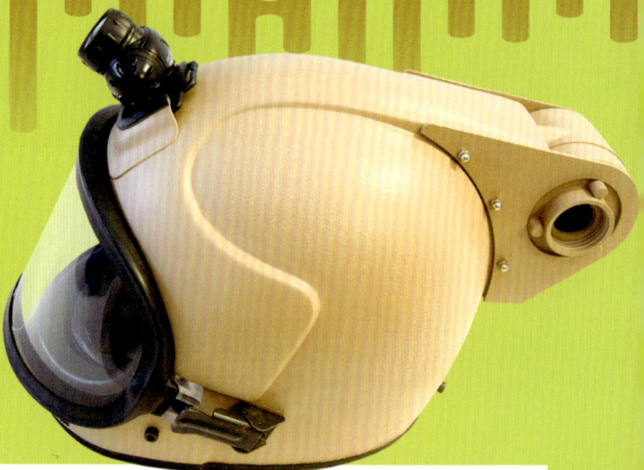

Engineering

1. Imagine you are an engineer. Your job is to create a new type of device to protect soldiers against IEDs.
2. Describe the device in detail and/or draw what it might look like. Be as detailed in your descriptions or drawings as you can.
3. Answer these questions:
   a) What will it look like?
   b) How will it work?
   c) How does the design help soldiers in battle?

Technology

1. Pick a weapon, such as a tank or airplane, and trace its development using research online.
2. Create a visual timeline from the weapon's first use until today.
3. On each timeline point, describe how the weapon changed or was used.

Math

1. Create a computer slideshow showing photos of different types of body armor used throughout history.
2. For each image, research the type of armor, who wears or wore it, when it is or was worn, and how it was designed to protect its wearer.

QUIZ to Take

1

How was chloroform administered to patients?

2

What type of clothing converts the Sun's energy into electricity?

3

What is an e-bomb?

4

What is Kevlar?

5

What material was used for tank armor during Operation Desert Storm?

6

What company created the "shockwave attenuation system"?

7

Why is fresh water important to a nuclear aircraft carrier?

8

What happens to kinetic energy in a bullet when its velocity increases?

9

What are two main types of body armor used today?

10

How does the interlocking stitching of bulletproof fabric minimize the impact of a speeding bullet?

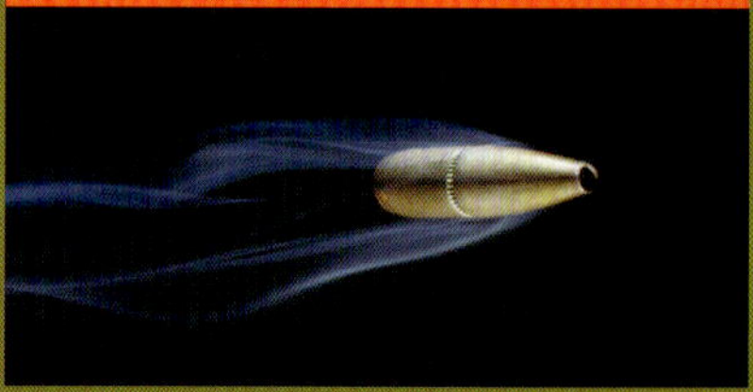

ANSWERS

1 The liquid slowly dripped into a cloth placed over the patient's nose **2** Solar uniforms **3** An electronic bomb that blasts computer systems with microwaves **4** A synthetic fiber of high tensile strength **5** Depleted uranium **6** Boeing **7** Fresh water in the reactor creates steam that powers the ship **8** It increases **9** Hard and soft **10** It scatters the energy over a wider area

KEY WORDS

anesthetics: substances that reduce sensitivity to pain and may cause unconsciousness

depleted uranium: a high-density type of uranium that can be sandwiched in between plates of steel tank armor

electromagnetic: magnetic energy such as light waves, X-rays, radio waves, and ultraviolet radiation

enzyme: a substance produced by cells that speeds up the chemical reactions necessary for life

exoskeleton: a skeleton or shell on the outside of something's body

infrared: a portion of invisible light in the electromagnetic spectrum between visible light and radio waves

intravenously: injected directly into veins

monocle: an eyeglass for one eye

photovoltaic: able to generate an electric current when exposed to visible sunlight

regime: the government in power

INDEX

LIGHTBOX

SUPPLEMENTARY RESOURCES

Click on the plus icon ⊕ found in the bottom left corner of each spread to open additional teacher resources.

- Download and print the book's quizzes and activities
- Access curriculum correlations
- Explore additional web applications that enhance the Lightbox experience

LIGHTBOX DIGITAL TITLES
Packed full of integrated media

VIDEOS

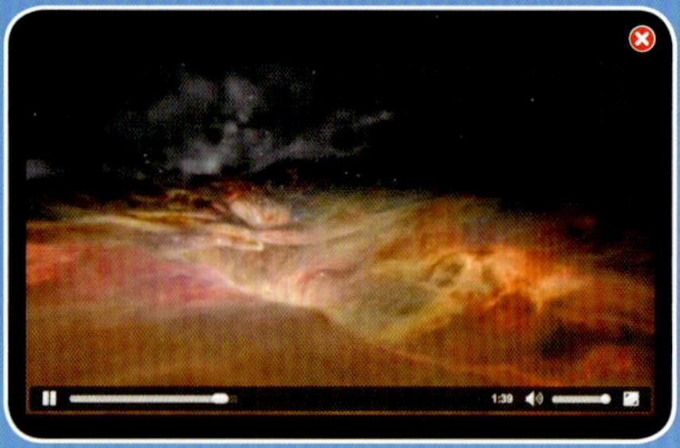

INTERACTIVE MAPS

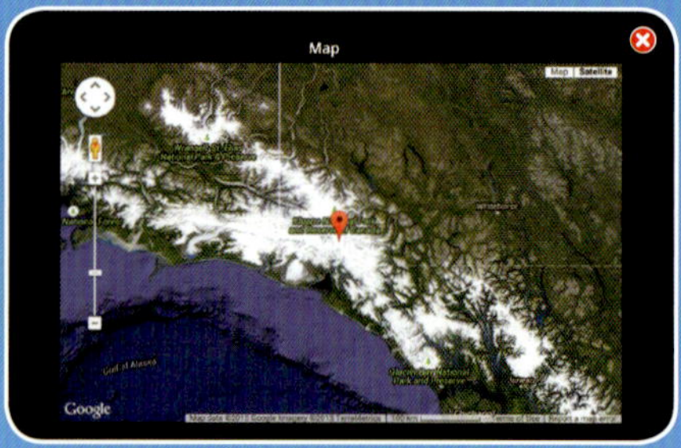

WEBLINKS

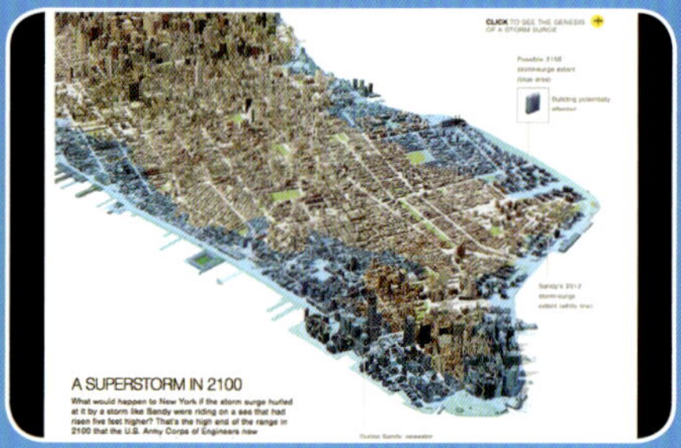

SLIDESHOWS

QUIZZES

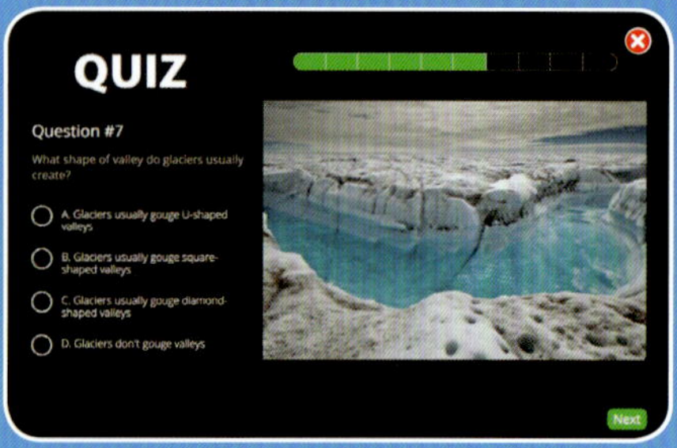

OPTIMIZED FOR

✔ TABLETS
✔ WHITEBOARDS
✔ COMPUTERS
✔ AND MUCH MORE!

Published by Smartbook Media Inc.
350 5th Avenue, 59th Floor
New York, NY 10118
Website: www.openlightbox.com

Library of Congress Control Number: 2019939916

ISBN 978-1-5105-4485-7 (hardcover)
ISBN 978-1-5105-4486-4 (multi-user eBook)

Printed in Guangzhou, China
1 2 3 4 5 6 7 8 9 0 23 22 21 20 19

062019
121218

Project Coordinator: John Willis
Art Director: Terry Paulhus

Photo Credits
Every reasonable effort has been made to trace ownership and to obtain permission to reprint copyright material. The publisher would be pleased to have any errors or omissions brought to its attention so that they may be corrected in subsequent printings.

The publisher acknowledges Alamy, Dreamstime, Getty Images, iStock, Newscom, the U.S. Army, and Wikimedia as its primary image suppliers for this title.

First published in 2017 by Mason Crest.